8 Reasons You'll Love Reading This Book:

1. You will learn the most important key to getting things done.

2. You will learn how to celebrate your successes and overcome your obstacles plus you'll discover how you can do so much more!

3. You will learn how to find more time in your day to do what you love.

4. You will learn creative ideas on how to get your name 'out there' and be seen.

5. You will learn how to get unstuck from what has been holding you back in life and in business.

6. You will learn how to create a clearer path to your success.

7. You will gain more insight on how to live a life you love and the secret to owning a business that lets you shine!

8. You will also learn how to get more money to invest in growing your business.

Each of these 8 reasons guarantee to help you instantly increase your impact, influence, and income!

Andrieka J. Austin, DBA The Socialprensita™

Correspondence concerning this book should be addressed to Andrieka J. Austin, DBA The Socialprenista™,

Contact: aj@thebossof.me

©2015 by Andrieka J. Austin, The Socialprenista™, Journey Girl, LLC Publishing Group and Journey Girl, LLC retains sole copyright to the contributions to this book. All rights reserved. No part of this book may be reproduced or transmitted in any form, except for the purpose of brief reviews, without the written permission of the publisher.

Published by Journey Girl Publishing Group and Journey Girl, LLC

E-mail: info@thesocialprenista.com

Website: www.TheSocialprenista.com

Questions or comments? Call 770-744-4475

All Socialprenista™ marks are trademarks of The Socialprenista™.

All Photos by G14 for The Studio Concept, Atlanta, GA

Photo Makeup: Sean B. Breezy Mac, www.TheUltraModel.com

All instructions in this book have been tested. Results from testing were incorporated into this book. Nonetheless, all recommendations and suggestions are made without guarantees on the part of Journey Girl Publishing Group. Because of differing tools, ingredients, conditions, and individual skills, the publisher disclaims liability for injury, losses, or other resulting damages or expense that may result from using the information in this book. Your use of reliance on the information in this book is at your own risk.

Austin, Andrieka J.

Secrets of a Socialprenista™ by Andrieka J. Austin

First Edition - 2015

1. Business 2. Professional Development 3. Business Development 4. Self-Help 5. Non-fiction 6. Entrepreneurship

ACKNOWLEDGEMENTS

Thanks to God, my inspiration and reason for writing this book.

To my Business Best Friend, Book Buddy and Success Coach, Mrs. T. Renee Smith, thank you for being the motivation I needed to get this message out into the world.

To my proofers, editors, focus group and feedback team {all in one}: Hannah Coker and Jamye Barnes, you guys ROCK! Thank you.

To all the women around the country who responded to my online survey about your business struggles, this book is my love letter and a box of {metaphorical} tissues for your years of tears!

To my book designer and other supporters for your encouragement and encouragement to complete this task, you have helped me become stronger than you know.

TABLE OF CONTENTS

PREFACE   1

INTRODUCTION   7

MISTAKE #1: PROCRASTINATION   9
See the value in what you have to offer and the difference it can make in someone else's destiny. There is only so much time we are allowed to exist on this earth. Someday is not a day on the calendar and it may never get here. Stop putting things off for later and move ahead!

MISTAKE #2: FEAR OF FAILING   20
Whether your fear is of success or failure, allow yourself to be who you truly are and move forward. Choosing not to do anything means you may (secretly) like things the way they currently are in your life and business. Before you determine your failure, first define your success!

MISTAKE #3: ATTEMPTING TO DO IT ALL   37
Despite your super-human strength, you cannot do it all by yourself. Knowing when to officiate and delegate allows you more freedom to seize the right opportunities. Aligning your business goals with your daily tasks determines successful investment of your time and money. List priority tasks and develop a team to support successful carryout the majority of those duties.

MISTAKE #4: BAD BRANDING   52
Once you know you, your business, and WHY you do what you do, brand it. Having confidence in your strengths and your business offerings allows you to focus on the specific needs of those you serve. You are your brand. Set yourself apart to stand out. Be creative and be you. Keep in mind your network reflects who you are, so recruit the efforts of brand ambassadors and mentors through social media supporters and other platforms.

MISTAKE #5: NOT KNOWING WHEN TO LET GO   66
Identify {and acknowledge} areas for personal and professional improvement to help you get to (and stay in) a place of clarity and focus.

MISTAKE #6: NO GUIDANCE   78
Get clear on what type of guidance you may need for your business. This process will allow you to discover your true strengths, see opportunities, and find peer-inspired success models for your journey.

MISTAKE #7: NO PASSION   89
Define your real passion and make no excuses! When you reveal your inner drive for the purpose, meaning, and the truth behind your business and life existence, you also begin to recognize the signs of passion for a cause that is true to you. Your true passion may only be an 'aha' away!

MISTAKE #8: NO FUNDS   100
Have an established business investment plan and a good, clear idea of funding criteria (and what you are willing to exchange or sacrifice) for the financial support of your business. Be able to speak of the investments you already have in place first as you evaluate your NEXT steps for growth in your business. Seek additional resources help keep on-track to meet your financial goals!

ABOUT THE AUTHOR   114

PREFACE

The passion behind the Socialprenista™ {pronounced Social•pre•nista} brand used to motivate and provide resources and training for empowering women entrepreneurs is multifaceted. For over a decade, I ran an organization called Journey Girl, LLC. This is something I created grassroots-style (from the ground-up) and it was designed as a series of workshops for mothers and daughters to start a dialogue on how to have better relationships with themselves and each other, specifically with beauty and self-esteem. With the success of the organization and ongoing brand recognition and growth (through tons of marketing and promoting), people started catching on to what we were doing in the community. We began getting requests to venture out into other states and territories and requests to franchise out the Journey Girl brand and success model.

Instead of branching out, I decided to switch my focus away from simply teaching workshops to coaching and training other women how to birth their vision and become successful at what they wanted to do and taking what they love to the next level. I started working with women entrepreneurs who had a vision to do something similar to the Journey Girl vision. I am now the person who assists with bringing things forth, based on what worked successfully under the Journey Girl brand.

I am a Certified Business and Life Coach for women entrepreneurs who are at a point where they are stuck and may not be making the amount of money they want to make. I share tactics that have successfully worked for me in the past, both personally and professionally. With this, I have helped other clients gain great results through my one-on-one business and life coaching sessions and live and virtual group workshops where I help women with specific aspects of their business. This helps them get clear, focused, and be held accountable for taking the next step.

I took what I did under the Journey Girl brand, which was considered a social enterprise. This is a modern-day version of a nonprofit organization (we were for-profit). I took what I learned as a successful social enterprise and I now tie it in with what I do today as a Business Coach and created the Socialprenista™ brand. It is a combination of being a woman entrepreneur with social enterprise experience on our side. The GREAT part of this new brand change is it also represents other great areas like speaking and sharing business knowledge. The new success of The Socialprenista™ brand is built on the solid foundation of the past personal and professional experience. With this, I now get to do what I LOVE, and I truly LOVE what I do! So, if I can do it, you can do it too ☺.

The following chapters are full of advice on lessons I've learned on the journey to growing a successful enterprise. To get the most out of this book, I encourage journal writing and note taking throughout our journey together as this will guide your mistake-avoiding process after you complete this book. Journals serve as your go-to source for guiding your thoughts and action-steps. It will come in handy at a later time when you may need to refer back to your insightful notes from the information shared and gleaned within these pages.

You can use this information to remind yourself of your plans and intentions for what next steps to take in your life and in your business. Throughout the book you will find checklists of inspirational and motivation. Check what is true for you today. Circle and make a note of the things you want to work on in your business and in life. Follow the instructions you have given yourself in each of your eight PINK-Print action steps at the end of each chapter. This will give you a map-like/PINK-Print (also referred to as a "blue print") of where you are and where you want (or need) to be in your life and/or your business. It will also open the door to help you establish mini-steps on exactly *how* you will get there. Use this information to help set your foundation and put your funding plan and other business/life goals in motion.

The goal of the methods shared in this book is to help professional business women with a strong desire to uncover the personal side of their professional struggles. This book provides insight on how to overcome the top mistakes women entrepreneurs make that keep them broke, stuck and struggling in their business. It will shed light on overcoming the obstacles of entrepreneurship and help women in business see those mistakes as an opportunity to grow and achieve more in their businesses. The strategies given enable entrepreneurs to handle these struggles in a positive, constructive way. My hope for each reader is she will implement a new action plan to help get unstuck and start moving forward in her life and in her business, knowing how to recognize and avoid these 8 mistakes once and for all.

I have received emails, phone calls, private LinkedIn and Facebook messages and requests for my business and life coaching services from aspiring and established women business owners who are on the verge of a melt-down. They are broke - unable to pay their staff or themselves. They are stuck - unsure of what moves to make, and they are struggling - only a few short days away from being forced to close their business doors forever.

After hearing their personal stories, I can always see right through to the issue. Most of their problems stem from not having a plan for how to properly start, sustain, and/or scale their business. Can you imagine all of the people who will be impacted if this were you, no longer in business as a result of the failure to create a simple, yet effective plan?

It truly hurts my heart to see and hear this scenario play out time and again. It does not have to be this way. It is as simple as deciding to invest in yourself and in your business by partnering with a support team of advisors, personal cheerleaders, and success coaches and developing a step-by-step process for taking your life and business to the next level.

Seeing and hearing about the personal and professional struggles of women in business, I conducted an e-mail survey of more than fifteen-hundred women entrepreneurs from around the world asking for a list of their top business struggles. [You can join the e-mail list too at www.TheSocialprenista.com]. These were to include anything taking their sleep at night, and those things that kept them stressing and fearful during the day.

Despite the number of personal and professional problems mentioned, I discovered a universally common list of topics most of the women surveyed shared, which include procrastination, fear of failing, attempting to do it all, bad branding, not knowing when to let go, no guidance, no passion, and no funds. As an overcomer and a self-proclaimed strategist in each of these areas, I have provided my own personal experience and helpful tips, tools, and tidbits of information for anyone dealing with these same issues but have a deep desire to get unstuck.

If you are a woman in business looking for a new way to get better results in your life and business, this book is for you. If you have an open heart about growth and change, you are in for a delightful journey. If you have an open mind about trying things a different way and building a support system to help you sustain, then read on. For any woman entrepreneur seeking business guidance, the following tips are guaranteed to help you reach your best potential and take your business to the next level. However, it is up to you to put this advice into action and be prepared to do the work! Without doing your part in this process, you will continue to make these common mistakes which ultimately affects your business, your health, your drive, and your ambition. This book is your guide to avoiding these mistakes once and for all.

To help you on your journey to getting unstuck, I will also introduce you to five self-empowerment tools all women are equipped with to accomplish any goal, task or job in her life and business which are Spirit, Mind, Heart, Mouth, and Actions. So, get ready!

I have spent the last several hundred days creating what I call a 'PINK-Print'. This is an effective planning and how-to guide for getting and keeping you unstuck, clear, and focused for the journey ahead. A part of the PINK-Print can be found at the end of each chapter. By the end of this book, you will have developed a working model of ideas to implement in your life and in your business to help you get unstuck and start moving forward step-by-step.

I have combined my decades of experience and education, tens of thousands of hours of training, coaching, reading and researching the information contained in this book. I have given my all to what I can now share with you. While this does not guarantee an overnight success, implementing the professional business and life coaching advice that follows can prove to be a very profitable way for you to plan your next steps to get from where you are to where you want to be in the immediate future. This expert advice can also serve as a great way to leave a legacy so your name and business efforts live on well after you do.

The advice I share with you on these pages will help you develop and utilize your own personal and professional brand when you put these ideas to effective and immediate use. They will allow you to obtain more freedom and fulfillment as you build a brighter future as the phenomenal business leader you are!

INTRODUCTION

Every intention to make a change in your life or business uses five self-empowerment tools. You were born with these tools and they will remain with you for the rest of your life. They are your spirit, mind, heart, mouth, and action. These go together to form a 5-step process for helping you make a decision to do things differently in your life and business. At the end of each chapter, you will form your own PINK-Print to help you make a plan to implement change in your life using each of these five areas.

The first empowerment tool is the Spirit. This is a when a thought, word or idea comes to you. It is one of the purest, most genuine parts of you. **Your next empowerment tool** is your Mind. What you think and feed yourself through your thoughts often manifest in your life. **Your third empowerment tool** is your Heart. This is when you are put on instinctive alert by a small whisper or a gentle tug that comes from within. **Your fourth empowerment tool** is your Mouth. What you profess out into the atmosphere often becomes your reality. **The fifth and final empowerment tool** is your Action. What you DO speaks louder than anything you can say, as this shows up as the 'fruit' in your life and is often what people witness seeing you do versus what they hear you saying. All five areas of the **spirit**, the **mind**, the **heart**, the **mouth**, and your **actions** go together to make lasting and permanent change!

Keep each tool in mind as you progress through **the top 8 mistakes mentioned** in this book that address making changes in your personal life to help you avoid professional struggles. The following pages will teach you how to avoid **procrastination** and see the value in what you have to offer and the difference it can make in someone else's life. You will move beyond your **fear of failing**, allow yourself to be who you truly are and press forward. You will finally stop **attempting to do it all** yourself. You will take an in-depth look at your life and in your business and what it takes to avoid **bad branding** in either of these. You will identify your areas of personal and professional areas to help you get (and stay) unstuck, never to make the mistake of **not knowing when to let go** again. Practicing the information shared, you are guaranteed to get clear on which guidance-type you seek and refrain from the mistake of having **no guidance** in your life or business. If you currently have **no passion** for what you do, you will once again be inspired to make things happen! You will discover the necessities for having an established business investment plan and steer clear of the **no funds** mistake once and for all.

This book includes eight sections which address each mistake individually, plus PINK-Print Points at the end of each section to help you begin developing your very own PINK-Print Action Plan for success.

When you decide to take action on the helpful tips, tools, and tidbits of great business advice shared in this book, you will increase your overall business impact, influence, and income for years to come. Happy reading! ☺.

MISTAKE #1: PROCRASTINATION

The work you put off today could potentially change someone's life in the future.
-Andrieka J. Austin

Procrastination sucks! It is plain and simple. It is a sign of laziness and a way of putting off your dreams for another day that is not promised to you. It is a way of telling yourself you feel unworthy, and it reveals your unspoken belief of not being good enough to impact or potentially change someone else's life. It is you doubting yourself and a way your mind has been trained to keep you stuck. It is a lack of your foundational belief in your ability to reach your goals and dreams of business success, and your way of remaining on pause.

Maybe you have decided to take a permanent break in the vision God promised you to grow a successful business and help change the world one life at a time. You might have decided against leaving a legacy for the next generation (as you promised yourself you would). Procrastination is the perfect way to stay stuck in a place you have a desire to move beyond. It is the perfect strategy to being exactly where you are now, this time next year.

My most recent encounter with procrastination was when I was required to submit a proposal to a long-time vision supporter. All I had to do was submit the necessary paperwork to in-turn receive a check (for several thousand dollars) which I have received each time I've applied for it. Well, procrastination kicked in and slowed things down a bit. I became so entangled with everything else going on around me, I missed the deadline and as a result I missed the money. While this was not my traditional routine way of doing things (it certainly did not look too good professionally), this event shifted my normal work timeline by several months and it enlightened me on just what procrastination actually means and how it affects our life and our businesses.

This was a lesson learned. The good news is I was given another chance to re-submit my information. The semi-okay news was I only had to wait a few months longer to re-send my information. I did so and overcame the chance of missing out on things ever happening again by developing a system I plan to always keep in place.

I started by getting everything I needed to re-send in one place for the new deadline I was given. Here's what I did; I put all the requested documents and paperwork in one place to help me prepare for an on-time send off. Once I completed the paperwork process, I compared it with a checklist of all of the items and documents that were being requested. This allowed me to ensure a successful delivery of all the material and information. I marked the date on my paper and dry erase calendar. I could have taken it a step further and even programmed it into my phone. I put this complete process as a priority task at the top of my to-do list each week leading up to the deadline. This served as a constant reminder the deadline was indeed approaching and that I needed to prepare myself (and my paperwork) to be READY to move with it!

I pre-addressed the mailing envelop I would eventually send everything in. By following this system, I submitted everything on time. My only hope was to then say a prayer, then call to verify all documents were received on-time and in order, and then to patiently wait for good results. I took 'baby steps' all the way up until the task was completed. This helped put off the temptation to do it later, and made the process short and sweet.

After all of this, here's what I learned:

Although it may be hard to accept, procrastination could mean a series of things:

1. It could possibly be a sign your business is not important to you.

2. It could mean you do not see the *value* in what you have to offer.

3. It may also mean you have not considered the significance your business products, or services will have in someone else's life.

A statement from The Goodie MoB (one of my favorite rap music groups) says, "*There is only so much time left in this crazy world.*" For me, this means it is time for you to get busy!

You can get things moving starting with an honest self-assessment to determine exactly where you are, versus where you want to be in your life and business. Next, create a list of ideas for how you can get out of your own way and actually achieve your goals and accomplish the things you realized (and finally admitted) you wanted based on your self-assessment results. Finally, stop hanging on to the what-ifs.

Believe me, it feels really good to get things done and check them off your list of 'things to do'. Remember, you have something to offer someone in need, so set your mind to get started and keep going until you reach each person seeking your help. Keep your head up, eyes forward, and hands uplifted. Stay focused and keep moving forward.

Regarding getting things done, here is a quick word of advice I call, the 'Get it off my desk!' work method. This system has proven effective time and again. The idea is it is always *someone's* turn to do their part in a major work project. In order to help bring everything together successfully, as soon as you get your part of the workload on your desk, do your part to 'get it off your desk'. That way, you know your work is done and you are free to move on to whatever comes next.

Here's a story: I had a friend who I labeled 'Queen Procrastinator'. She is the mother of two. Her children were attending elementary and middle school. For nearly a decade she has consistently told me, her family, friends (and herself) the story of "someday" what she was planning to accomplish. She often mentioned her dream of 'someday' going back to school, and 'someday' hosting a conference for women. This, she promised would all happen "once her children were in school" (her words!). Her eldest child graduated is now halfway through college, and her youngest child is currently successfully making his way through junior high.

During a recent phone conversation, she had begun her usual storytelling of 'someday' what she hoped to achieve in her life. At that moment, the Business Coach in me kicked in, and I kindly reminded her of her eldest child's recent graduation, and how her youngest child is quickly approaching the end of his school day journey as well. The phone fell silent. She was speechless. She began silently weeping. She felt guilty and ashamed of putting her dreams off for so long. She believed time had passed her by. It immediately became clear to her, her 'someday' had come and gone months, if not years ago. She had finally run out of excuses for what she had 'someday' planned to do.

The lesson I hope you've learned from this story is when you keep putting things off for someday, your things-to-do list (someday) continues to expand. You must be honest with yourself to know when to STOP. When enough is enough. My advice to you is, it is time to stop dreaming and start doing. Take a moment and consider your impact on the lives of those you influence by not getting started on what you've been called to do. People are waiting on you. Really. You provide a service they do not even know exists yet.

Most importantly, what you have to offer is something someone needs. Think about it. Someone somewhere is waiting on you to make your next move. While you may be waiting on something, someone is waiting on you. It's time to get it together and give the people what they need to make it to the next level in their life and in their business.

Years ago someone told me If I did not walk in my destiny of serving and empowering others, there would be thousands of women who would never receive what they needed for their own destiny. Imagine the remorse, guilt, and stress I felt in that moment (and still do!). It was then that I immediately surrendered my laziness, doubts, fears and comfort. I finally surrendered and said "Yes!" to dedicating my time, talents, gifts, skills, and attention to helping women through the journey of entrepreneurship for generations to come.

Despite the feeling of the proverbial weight of the world being upon my shoulders, it is my life's mission to do what I have been called to do during my time here on this precious earth. At this time, I ask you to accept this spiritual transfer of energy (and pressure) as I share with you my own sense of urgency for you to get started and make things happen. Remember, someone somewhere is waiting on you!

To help you keep going with this process, here are a few points of guidance and action steps

- Start with a CAN DO attitude.

- Focus specifically on what you have to offer through your business, and how it will benefit others.

- Decide <u>today</u> to take one small step, execute your plan of action, and move your business forward.

- Get the job done by pursuing your mission and vision to leave a legacy for generations to come.

- Keep the momentum going by developing small day-by-day action steps (also note how you intend to implement what needs to be done in your business).

- Get ready to take A-C-T-I-O-N!

- Use what you have.

- Start where you are.

We all procrastinate and have (lame) reasons for not doing some things. Most of us put things off because we have other things to do. Things like checking your online status, keeping track of the number of 'likes' we get from an old picture we posted, clicking on the picture of our friend's new baby or watching dancing cat videos, etc.

Think about it, everything I just listed takes just as much effort as opening up your computer program to start writing your first (or next) book. It also requires the same effort to start researching business growth ideas, or making that important phone call you've been putting off. However, if you want to appear lazy, keep social *not*-working and put your dreams off for another day.

I heard someone say 'someday' is not an actual day on the calendar. You can start today by leaving a legacy and making your mark on the world. Present your gift to those who are patiently waiting to learn and receive the goods and services your business produces. Go ahead. Hit the 'play' button on your life. No more waiting. No more excuses. No more putting it off. Go do it!

Let's Recap...

1. Procrastination sucks!

2. Your business should be important to you.

3. Don't be a Queen Procrastinator.

4. When you put things off, your to-do list continues to expand.

5. Someone somewhere needs you.

6. Have a CAN DO attitude.

7. Get started and keep going.

8. To get things done, get it off your desk!

9. Start where you are.

10. Use what you have.

11. The work you don't do determines your business success or failure.

12. 'Someday' is not a day on the calendar, so it will never come.

Here is an Inspiration + Affirmation Checklist:

Place a check by what is true for you today. Circle what you want to work on. Make a note of it in your personal journal.

- ☐ **My business is important to me**

- ☐ **My mission is important to me**

- ☐ **I see the value in what I have to offer**

- ☐ **I know and accept the significance of my gift in someone else's life through my business products/services**

- ☐ **I acknowledge and understand there is only so much time left to answer the call and complete my business/life mission**

- ☐ **I am moving out of my own way**

- ☐ **I will avoid the "what if" mode**

- ☐ **I am FOCUSED**

- ☐ **I am ready for ACTION**

PINK-Print Point 1: Decide.

Your first PINK-Print action step is to **stop putting things off for later** and make a **decision** today.

Remember, **the 5 empowerment tools**: **Spirit** {when a thought, word or idea comes to you. It is one of the purest, most genuine parts of you}, **Mind** {what you think and feed yourself through your thoughts often manifest in your life, **Actions** {what you DO speaks louder than anything you can say, as this shows up as the 'fruit' in your life and is often what people witness seeing you do versus what they hear you saying, **Mouth** {what you profess out into the atmosphere often becomes your reality}, and **Heart** {when you are put on an instinctive alert by a small whisper or a gentle tug that comes from within}.

All five areas of the **spirit**, the **mind**, the **heart**, the **mouth**, and your **actions** go together to make lasting and permanent change!

Answer the following questions in your journal:

1. What task has been nagging at you to get it done?

2. How do you *think* you can get this specific task accomplished?

3. How will you *feel* when this task is finally complete?

4. What are you *saying* (aloud or to yourself) about accomplishing this task?

5. What is your next small step to get things done?

6. What will you *do* TODAY to get this task complete? When will you get started?

MISTAKE #2:
Fear Of Failing

"You must go through failure to get to success."
-Jenni Pulos

Even if you fail at something, what is the worst thing that could happen? Honestly, think about it. If you've ever failed at something, it is possible that the worst has already occurred. The hard part is over, and it is behind you.

I believe that a failure is simply a way of allowing you to see what ideas and techniques did not work right for you the first time. Failure also gives you the chance to make a few adjustments while you pick yourself up and go at it again.

One of the best things you can do for yourself before going for any of your goals is to clearly define what failure means to you. Have an idea of what things would look like for you if you were to fail at something. Then, turn and run in the opposite direction! It is that simple. Your dreams are too important to give up on the first try. You must keep trying.

So what you are afraid of failing. Who isn't? Who do you know that has tried anything that was hard and did not fail before finding their formula for success? Who says failing at anything is a bad thing?

Don't beat yourself up when it comes to trying and not succeeding one or two times. If you tend to carry the "failure" with you forever, that is not being fair to yourself.

You must admit you are human; you will make mistakes. Sometimes you will not succeed at what you set out to accomplish as it relates to your dreams, your goals, your vision, or your mission for your business. But, it is okay.

It hurts to think a business you have worked so hard to create could possibly end up as a flat out failure. It's scary to think that your big dream or vision may not work out, despite all the great things you have planned.

Why would you set yourself up to fail, right? Wrong. Although you know that failure is a realistic possibility and you are putting a lot on the line still go ahead and give it chance. Take a risk. Go for it. Do not set yourself up to fail, but take the chance to see if your business idea (or business) is a good one (or not).

Think about it. More than likely, this will not be your first time failing at something in your life. I am almost certain you can recall a time when you have failed at something before. But, you recovered. The key point here is you recovered, and now you are in a position to start fresh (and do it all over again). But, this time you are smarter and you know exactly what to do (and what not to do). There are lessons that you have learned. Now you have a clearer vision and a plan for moving forward with your goals and dreams. So what if you fail?

If you are worried about what others will say, get over it. Who are they to judge what you have dreamed about and hoped for, for so long?

Who are you to let anyone stand in the way of you fulfilling that dream? It is your dream. If what you want lines up with what your heart says, who cares what family and friends say or think, right?

Many people will try to transfer their own personal worries, fears, and insecurities onto you. Don't let them. It is normal to expect (and even accept) some criticism, but you cannot allow that to stop you from moving forward in your own life or business.

I mentioned before there are thousands of people waiting on you to 'do your thing' before they can do theirs. They need your permission, via your business products and services.

With this information alone, it no longer matters what anyone else thinks.

People will talk anyway. Let them talk. You might as well make sure they are talking about your success and how you overcame your fear of failure and kept pushing on.

Here are a few things to consider when dealing with the naysayers and those who do not fully understand who you are, what you do, and *why* you do what you do.

1. We have graduated high school already. You are officially part of the "in crowd" with the popular kids, so stop looking for "their" approval. Who are they?

2. Let those you serve testify and attest to your work. Let your work and service define who you are and exactly what you do. Let your work and the results you help your <u>paying</u> customers achieve, speak for you.

3. Stop complaining. No more focusing on the negative. Remember what you feed grows.

4. Know who you are and choose to live and operate in the value you bring to those who are fans of your work.

5. Ask yourself *why* you care what "they" say.

6. Stand firm and confidently in what you do. There is a scripture which mentions *"Being confident of this, that He who began a good work in you will continue it on to the day of Christ Jesus."* (Philippians 1:6)

7. Know for sure exactly *why* you do what you do.

8. Speak to the impact of the "what", "why", and 'how" you do what you do. To offer even more support, back up this by showing the numbers of clients or customers you've served, testimonials, and who's been impacted by your products and services.

9. You can always survey your clients to see if they are satisfied with you, your products and services, and ask them for their feedback and tips on how you can serve them better. This can work well for you and your business. Especially since your clients are the ones writing the checks!

10. Understand everyone will not like your idea, and be okay with that fact. Expect it. Get over it. This is not your issue (so do not take it on as one). It is their issue, so let them deal with it. Your job is to simply stay focused and keep with the mission of your business by increasing your overall impact, influence, and income! That's my motto.

While failing, and accepting failure seems devastating. In order to know if you have failed at something (specifically in business), you should also have an idea of what success looks like and what it means to you. This way, you will know what it looks like when you get there! And remember, if you keep trying, you will indeed eventually get there.

For example, you may envision success as having a business that provides the income you need to replace, compete with, and/or surpass your annual past (or current) corporate salary.

Success for you may be a life full of peace and the freedom to spend your time and your days however you choose. These instances may sound quite simple to some, but may require a big leap for others. Either way, however <u>you</u> define success is worth going for it!

Here's my story:

From elementary school to college, I consistently remained on the 'A/B Honor Roll' for making good grades in school. I received awards and positive recognition for having excellent study habits and an above average comprehension of school subjects.

In college, I made plans to speed up the process to graduate early by taking on more classes. This decision backfired. I received my first official "F" as a letter grade. Now, I did not set out to make this grade. However, I did ignore my instincts and that little voice within whispering, "you are doing too much". I put a lot of extra, unnecessary stress upon myself by taking on the extra workload of classes and additional responsibilities. I did more than was required and as a result, I became mentally, physically, and emotionally overwhelmed.

I noticed my stress levels (and my blood pressure) from the pressures I put on myself to over-accomplish the day-to-day demands of my in-school, and after-school activities (i.e., homework, studying for tests, and still making good grades, and running a business full-time.).

I decided to take a step back and acknowledge what I already knew to be true on a deeper level. I made a decision to accept the fact I could not keep this up. For the first time in my life, I would receive a failing letter grade. I instantly made the choice to (humbly) receive and be okay with that.

The Bible mentions, '*No temptation has overtaken you except such as common to man; but God is faithful, who will not allow you to be tempted beyond what you are able , but with the temptation will also make the way of escape, that you may be able to bear it.*' (1st Corinthians 10:13). However, sometimes we take it upon ourselves to overdo certain things in our lives and in our business. These things can overwhelm us and ultimately end up as what we consider to be failures.

Now knowing my struggles in this area, I encourage you to take a moment to evaluate where you are in your life and in your business. Take note of what you are doing too much of and the extra things you have allowed yourself to take on. Pay close attention to how you are feeling deep down. Focusing on how you feel will let you know if you are setting yourself up for failure. Be honest with yourself and decide what you may need to do in this moment. What do you need to do to keep from failing?

Also, decide how you want to fail and note, there is a difference between a **private** and a **public** failure.

Private failure is when you fail alone. For example, if you are a small, home-based business with no employees, more than likely, you work alone. When you try something that does not work (most of the time) only *you* know about it.

On the other side of things, is a *public* failure. This is when you fail with the whole world watching. It's also what we are most used to hearing so much about in the media.

For example, when a celebrity does something that goes against what we believe is 'the success factor', it is made out to be a big deal. It is a catch twenty-two of sorts. On one hand celebrities are viewed as successful. However, as soon as he/she makes a mistake in our eyes, we immediately see them as a failure.

As we discussed earlier, success and failure are terms that are personal to each individual. You may look at yourself as a failure for that small project that did not go well (which only you know about in the privacy of your own home office).

However, the celebrity may not view himself or herself as a failure. He or she may choose to see things as a small "mistake", a pivot or a learning experience *not* to do something.

In this case, there are two different definitions of 'failure' and 'success' at work here. It is all about one's mindset. Plus, it is up to you to choose which way you'll choose to see things (failure or success).

Think about it, many successful people may not have found their own "success factor" if they would not have tried, failed, and repeated the process several times before getting it right.

Once you find out what does not work, you are then at liberty to begin the process again and doing things better this time. Set yourself up for success by having a better plan and a bigger goal in mind.

You now have a clearer vision for your success with these newly revised steps in place to help get you to the next level.

Whether public or private, I have defined failure as giving up or not doing anything with what you have. When you have been inspired with a great idea or an amazing new concept and you are too afraid to give it a try, that is considered a failure to me.

When I first started my business, I noticed when I spent most of my time in what I call my "dream phase" (which translates into not actually doing anything with my ideas), someone else would come up with that same idea and put it out into the world themselves.

For instance, about fifteen years ago, I had a dream of a hand-held apparatus that was used to spray make-up on the face. I awoke and remembered the dream vividly. I even sketched out the picture of how this gadget would look (the same way I'd seen in my dreams). Then, I tucked the drawing and my dream notes away thinking, "Wow! That was an awesome dream and such a unique new tool to introduce to the make-up industry (and I do not even wear make up!)".

Because the idea was so futuristic to me, I could not wrap my mind around exactly how I could (secretly) share my idea without someone else stealing it. So I hid it away for safe keeping (so I thought) and never did anything with it.

Fast-forward a few years later, turn on any television channel and you'll now see a commercial with a model sitting in a chair while a Make-up

Artist airbrushes make-up on her face by using the same tool that appeared to me in my dreams decades ago, but I never did anything with the idea. Someone else did.

How disappointing. You know this is the thought that played over and again each time I see that commercial.

I remember my dream and my drawing/sketch and how much money I could have at this very moment by selling my brilliant idea to the right person in the makeup-thingy-making industry.

I still often wonder if I showed my drawing to a Judge, would he/she believe me and award me a percentage of the fortune being made off of "my idea"! How embarrassing. How dare I even attempt to say "they stole my idea" when I did not have the guts to do anything with it?

By using something as simple as starting the research process on the idea, I would have at least been making the first step to move forward with it.

Sometimes, a failure is seen as a failure, whether you feel like you let yourself or someone else down. Or like me, you may even experience feelings of sadness, disappointment, shame, or guilt as a result of the idea you never acted on either out of failure or fear.

From my years of working with women entrepreneurs, I have found there are several reasons why people might decide not to try to move forward with certain things in their life or business. When you avoid taking a chance or a risk, it could be an expression you secretly are comfortable with the things in your life and your business right now. It's your way of choosing NOT to move forward.

The most common reason many people choose not to move forward is fear. But not just fear, the fear of failure. This means being afraid of what *could* go wrong.

Fear of failure could also be disguised as a deeper fear. A fear of success. This is when everything is going right, but a person is lingering on what the moment of success could possibly bring along with it in terms of responsibilities and expectations.

For example, you might be afraid of taking on a new project in your business. You might consistently ask yourself, "What if things go wrong?" This is a perfect example of a fear of failure or "What if I can't handle the new responsibility and expectations that come with taking on a new project or assignment?" This is an example of fear of success.

Now, let's reverse these thought processes. What if you take on the new project and you succeed? What if everything goes according to your plan and turns out to be your best project yet, and you get amazing results?

While either of these scenarios may have you more than a little afraid of what comes next, just remember that in most situations you may never know the outcome. It's not until you get past those feelings of uncertainty and being unsure and decide to try it anyway you may discover what you could have done all along, despite your fears.

Be bold and believe in yourself. Imagine fully embracing all you are truly meant to do, be, and become.

Taking on a new task or journey can be an intimidating and enlightening experience. Just remember to keep looking straight ahead and move forward, thinking of all the perks that will come with success ☺.

Be mindful another person's definition of success or failure may not match your own.

When you take on the title of 'failure', accept the fear that comes along with it.

This also means you may feel less than, no good, and unworthy. Take the information you've learned from this book and give yourself a chance at succeeding *before* you consider yourself, your project, or your business a failure.

Define success and failure on your own terms. Remember, success is something you work toward. You may not be exactly where you want to be yet, but with your own clearly defined meaning of the terms 'failure' and 'success', you will recognize it once you get there. This will mean you no longer make the 'fear of failure' mistake.

Before we end, four things I have found to be life-long lessons when facing a fear of a certain level of success are:

1. Your past failures will always help you remember where you came from (specifically the bad or unsuccessful times).

2. Past experiences allow you to avoid the previously mentioned bad or unsuccessful times. This will keep you moving forward and strengthen your desire to succeed even more.

3. The encounters that take place during the journey help you understand what it is like to be in unsuccessful circumstances. This can serve as your driving force to continue on (and pay it forward along the way by helping others).

4. Trust and continue to believe in the guidance and inspiration that brought you success. Repeat the process and you will consistently increase your success rate!

I hope this helps. Let's keep moving forward together.

Let's Recap...

1. Never fear failure.

2. It is NOT your first time.

3. Get OVER what "They" say.

4. Define your OWN success.

5. Remember MY mistakes.

6. Know the two failure types.

7. See how failure is *really* defined.

8. Reverse the fear of failure process.

9. Believe in you.

10. With failure the worst is OVER.

Here is an Inspiration + Affirmation Checklist:

Place a check by what is true for you today. Circle what you want to work on. Make a note of it in your personal journal.

☐ I am open and free to be me

☐ I have defined what success is (and will look like) for me

☐ I understand I cannot live my life in fear of failure

☐ I know who I am and I acknowledge her

☐ I am moving forward and changing only what I know I can

☐ I have a vision for my life to be better in some way each day

☐ I am not concerned with what "they" say. It is not my business anyway

☐ I will not give up. I am living the life I desire to live, no matter what

PINK-Print Point 2:
Define.

Your second PINK-Print action step is to **define** your success.

Remember, **the 5 empowerment tools**: **Spirit** {when a thought, word or idea comes to you. It is one of the purest, most genuine parts of you}, **Mind** {what you think and feed yourself through your thoughts often manifest in your life, **Actions** {what you DO speaks louder than anything you can say, as this shows up as the 'fruit' in your life and is often what people witness seeing you do versus what they hear you say, **Mouth** {what you profess out into the atmosphere often becomes your reality}, and **Heart** {when you are put on an instinctive alert by a small whisper or a gentle tug that comes from within}.

All five areas of the **spirit**, the **mind**, the **heart**, the **mouth**, and your **actions** go together to make lasting and permanent change!

Answer the following questions in your journal:

1. How do you define success?

2. What does success look like for you in your life/business?

3. How do you *feel* about your own current success?

4. What are you *saying* (aloud or to yourself) about your future success in your life/business?

5. What will you *do* TODAY to live out your definition of success?

MISTAKE #3: Attempting To Do It All

Hey Superwoman!

Always remember you are human. No matter what you may think (or what anyone may tell you), you are not invincible. You cannot be and do *everything* it takes on your own to run a successful business.

I once heard someone say, "'You can have it all, but you cannot do it all" (at least not all at once). I believe this is true. It helps to get help. But first, you must know when to officiate and when to delegate certain tasks, duties, and responsibilities in your business. You have to know which opportunities to take advantage of, how they meet your overall business goals, and if you should be the one who carries them out or if you should simply pass the task on to another capable person on your team.

Do what I call the F-A-R-T system and Finish (complete what is required), Assign (pass the task on to an assistant, volunteer, or intern), Research (look more into what is needed to move forward), or Terminate (end the life cycle of) each document that comes across your desk. You need to FART and move on.

Surprisingly enough, sometimes it feels good to let go and let someone else take the reins!

To get a clear picture and a better focus on which tasks to do (file/attend) and which to pass on (refer/trash), follow these few easy steps:

1. Write down the details of the task. This helps "empty your brain" and put things on paper along with a few action steps. List what you do (and do not) want to do when it comes to carrying out the task.

2. After you make a list of what must get done, re-read the list and specify the things you love (and do not love) to do concerning the task at-hand. You can start this process off by having a question and answer session with yourself regarding what it is about each specific task you love to do. Be specific.

3. Question (and answer) yourself in writing on whether each task you've listed identifies with the goals, the mission, and the vision model of your business. If so, how does each task align accordingly?

4. Next, ask yourself the most important question; *Why* is each task you've listed *so* important (or not) to you and your business?

5. Be specific. Next question; Are these tasks a need-to-have or a want-to-have in your business? {Make a note of your answer next to each task on your list}.

6. Include bullet points on how each task is (or is not) in alignment with your business focus and what you can potentially learn or benefit from by Finishing, Assigning, Researching or Terminating each task/assignment.

7. Finally, consider if or when you (or someone else) complete each task how the completed task will **make more money** for you in your business. If this question cannot be answered for each item on your list, then it is definitely time to terminate the task.

If anyone knows what it is like to wear many (and by many, I mean all) of the "hats" required as an entrepreneur, I do. From the moment you open your eyes in the morning, you have business on the brain.

Starting the day with checking e-mails, taking phone calls from people (who you **hope** are) calling to do business with you and not "virtual tire kickers" calling to "get information". With each moment, you are using a portion of your (limited) time checking your Facebook or LinkedIn messages, posting an update to your "status" (and scrolling your friends' news feeds **somehow** slips in there too!), tweeting and blogging are all now also a part of your daily agenda.

By this time, you are mentally and physically drained. You have not even completely dressed yourself (or gotten out of bed for that matter). Not to mention, you have not spent any *quality*, valuable time with yourself doing things like praying, meditating, exercising, self-grooming, hygiene-building, or eating a well-balanced meal to help you get your day off to a good start.

Come to think of it, did you really even get the full eight hours of good night's sleep as recommended for good health and overall well-being?

Speaking of well-being, I started working to make money for myself when I was fourteen years old. I was required to have what was known as a Worker's Permit, which gave me legal permission to work until a certain time of the day.

Since I was still a freshman in high school at the time, the number of hours I could work and the amount/type of work I could do was limited.

Knowing this, my goal was to get to work as early as possible (usually right after school), and to stay as late as I could, even if only a few minutes before I was scheduled to leave. I did this routine day-after-day and month-after-month.

At one of my first jobs, the hiring store manager (for some reason) did not check my onboarding paperwork. He assumed I was older than I really was (I'm guessing it was my maturity level) and he scheduled me to work up until the store's closing time, which was several hours beyond my approved permit's limit.

According to my work permit, I could not be scheduled to work past 7:00pm on a school night. The store closed at 10:00pm. The manager did not check my records for several months. I said nothing to bring this to his attention because I was enjoying working longer hours, making my own money and getting better at my job (I was a checkout cashier at a local grocery store)!

One day after arriving at work, I went to open my register and the checkout lane to start receiving customers. Then, it happened. Seemingly out-of-the-blue I began to feel sharp cramps in my chest and the muscles in my chest.

In an attempt to relieve the pain, I massaged the tired, stiff areas where I felt the pain. I leaned against the counter and my head slowly went down near the conveyor belt, and BOOM! My legs went weak and I blacked out. My body crashed. I could not move. I could not lift my head.

To this day, I still do not remember how I made it to the emergency room of the hospital that night. But I will forever remember the feeling of being beyond exhausted from overworking.

The memory of this incident will be forever etched in my mind as a reminder of what can happen when I (or anyone else) attempts to do it all. This experience taught me how important it was to allow your body and your mind to REST.

Take time off. Share responsibilities with teammates who support you, and want to see you succeed. This is the same message I want to share with you.

Just like my work experience during my younger years, I quickly discovered the entrepreneur's journey is tough. But, somehow it is also worth it.

While you may want to, it does not make sense to attempt to do everything on your own you do not have to. I teach my clients how to create their own volunteer internship program (and get free help without hiring!).

Together, we go through the steps to creating a (free) virtual team of helpers and supporters to assist them throughout the growth of their business.

Get creative and design a Volunteer Internship Program [VIP] for students or stay-at-home-moms looking for opportunities to serve. I conducted an interview with a self-proclaimed "Career Intern" and she shared some helpful advice on how to attract and retain ideal candidates for your VIP team, along with priceless tips to significantly enhance the work experience you provide those who sign on to help and support your business mission and vision.

Also, places like colleges, universities, and volunteer websites are great for scouting interns, apprentices, and virtual assistants. These resources are available to you for finding free or low-cost help for yourself and your business so you can take a load off.

As an energy-booster, here are 18 helpful tips from the VIP course I use (and a few tips from the interview with a professional intern) for getting started and building a great foundation for a Volunteer or Internship Program [VIP] to bring in more (free) help for your business:

1. It's best to start out knowing your work style. Are you easy to work with (or around)? Would YOU work for you?

2. List your top ten business priorities. Narrow them down to the top three and pass this list along to someone who's capable of carrying these details out.

3. Layout the duties and tasks required to complete the top 3 tasks you will be delegating to your team. Describe your directions in a step-by-step method to ensure successful completion of each task.

4. It's good to create rules around how to complete each task. Be sure to be specific on the consequences involved for tasks that are not completed as well.

5. When you are ready and able to delegate and let go of some of your workload, things start to feel lighter. Allow yourself to trust the person you gave the (detailed) task list to. Be confident he or she is competent and will carry out the job the way you clearly instructed, and you will be okay with the results (even if things may not be done in the *exact* way you would do them). Simply be open to the work being d-o-n-e, and not perfect.

6. Now that you have decided which of your top 3 priorities will be delegated, select your most important task.

7. No matter which assignment(s) you decide to delegate, be sure to focus each one around the overall mission and vision of your business.

8. Create strategic goals and define the desired outcome of each task. It is now time to show what the success of this project looks like.

9. At this point, it would also be helpful to create task templates, handouts, and other supporting materials to go along with each task assignment to help your VIPs carry things out correctly.

10. Pre-set a clear turn-around time for each task's start and completion lifecycle and deadline.

11. Sync each task's start time within 3 days of your VIPs onboarding start date. Schedule each task end time to occur at least one week before the end of your VIP program.

12. Once you have designed each task's goals and shared your ideal completion results, plan on bringing one volunteer, intern, or virtual assistant on board to help you complete the specifics of the tasks you listed.

13. Divide lengthy task duties into smaller bits of tasks to be shared among your team of VIPs. Coordinate multiple VIPs to increase work production and speed up task completion time for larger tasks.

14. Set a schedule to meet with your VIPs individually or as a group at least once-a-week throughout the length of your VIP program to set up dates on task progress and evaluations. Leave time for feedback from your team during these meetings.

15. Assign your highest priority task first. Share your written out walk-through of the procedure and methods for a successful task completion process.

16. Encourage daily (or every-other-day) check-ins with task/assignment questions via e-mail or in a quick chat-by-phone meeting. This makes staying on task and staying focused a lot easier for you and your VIPs.

17. Don't stop there. Plan out additional tasks and assignments for current and future VIPs. As you know, an entrepreneur's work never ceases. There is always something to do and you can always use the free help for sharing your workload.

18. At the end of each task, give your VIPs the opportunity to share improvement suggestions, comments, and feedback for how to make things run smoother on future tasks and assignments.

19. To help keep the flow of your VIP program going, create a referral system for teammates with interested colleagues, friends, and associates who they can introduce to the program. This will allow for a consistent flow of (free) help, keeping you in the mode you do not have to do everything on your own!

Being able to share your workload by having good help is the best way to avoid being overwhelmed, overworked, and experiencing flat-out exhaustion (like I did!). Following these eighteen tips should give you a better idea for determining where to invest your time and money when it comes to tasks, duties, assignments, and responsibilities in running your business.

Laying out how you wish each task to be completed is the start of a systematic approach to getting things done (without attempting to do it all on your own!). Take advantage of the resources and all forms of free help you can get to help run your business more efficiently and effectively. This ensures your greater business and life sustainability and sanity all at the same time.

Let's Recap...

1. Despite your super-human strength, you cannot be it all and do it all in your own in business.

2. "Empty your brain" by writing out what you want and why you want it, plus how it aligns with your business goals and focus.

3. Design your own VIPs to lighten your load.

4. Focus your VIP projects on the overall mission and vision of your business.

5. Provide detailed step-by-step instructions on what a successful project outcome looks like.

6. Have a goal deadline and an end-of-project date in mind before going in.

7. Pep things up with a weekly meeting or chat with your VIPs to ensure things are staying on task and on-target to meet your deadline.

8. Get feedback and suggestions from your current team on how to improve the program.

9. Be willing to share the workload.

Here is an Inspiration + Affirmation Checklist:

Place a check by what is true for you today. Circle what you want to work on. Make a note of it in your personal journal.

- ☐ I acknowledge that I am not a super human. I will not attempt to be super-human

- ☐ I know when (and what work) to delegate

- ☐ I have a current list of my business goals, as it relates to my business mission/vision

- ☐ I know what I want for my life and my business, plus it aligns with all of my goals

- ☐ I know when and where to invest my time to best benefit my business

- ☐ I give detailed project completion information to my support team

- ☐ I assign all projects with a plan for a successful completion

- ☐ I have pep-talks with my team to boost morale and success rates

- ☐ **My to-do tasks are prioritized and can be clearly explained and delegated to my team**

- ☐ **I am not attempting to do it all on my own**

PINK-Print Point 3: List.

Your third PINK-Print action step is to

list and dish

your top business/life priorities.

Remember, **the 5 empowerment tools**: **Spirit** {when a thought, word or idea comes to you. It is one of the purest, most genuine parts of you}, **Mind** {what you think and feed yourself through your thoughts often manifest in your life, **Actions** {what you DO speaks louder than anything you can say, as this shows up as the 'fruit' in your life and is often what people witness seeing you do versus what they hear you say, **Mouth** {what you profess out into the atmosphere often becomes your reality}, and **Heart** {when you are put on an instinctive alert by a small whisper or a gentle tug that comes from within}.

All five areas of the **spirit**, the **mind**, the **heart**, the **mouth**, and your **actions** go together to make lasting and permanent change!

Answer the following questions in your journal:

1. What are your top business goals?

2. How do you *think* you can achieve these goals?

3. What do you *feel* is the next best step for getting the job done?

4. How will you *ask* others for their help with this?

5. What will you *do* TODAY to make this a top priority?

MISTAKE #4: BAD BRANDING

When focusing on branding yourself as a woman business owner and a leader in your industry, there are a few key qualities you must possess. Basic, personal characteristics like maintaining a high level of integrity and honesty will get you a long way. A positive boost in self-esteem and confidence, positive personality and an optimistic outlook on business and life are traits that will serve you well.

I co-authored a book with a group of business women called, *Just Me; The Business Woman's Personal Branding Guide*. In it, I share how as a professional business woman, you are your brand. As a business woman, you represent your individual brand both personally and professionally. Your brand starts with what you wear and continues with how you carry yourself.

Your brand precedes you. It represents a professional snapshot of you and your business expertise. The bottom line is, you are a representation of yourself and your business. Your brand can ultimately determine your business success or failure.

Your brand can be reflected in a logo, a symbol similar to the "Golden Arches" that represent a well-known fast food chain. Although the arches do not spell out the word "hamburger" -- except in our minds-- they are a symbol which makes it impossible not to think of French fries and a soft drink.

Branding is your image, reputation, mark, "stamp", leverage, and/or your own "*you*-niqueness" representing you personally, and your company professionally. Branding is something you find, define, and own as a part of your personal and your business' professional representation. It reflects what you tell people you are good at doing and what someone thinks of as your particular area of expertise, along with what you want your business to be well-known for.

As a professional speaker, author, entrepreneur and a professional business woman I know I will always be my brand. It did not take me long to realize this. I carry each of these titles, plus that of a passion-led Business Coach as I facilitate training workshops on topics that pertain to the personal and professional development for women small business owners.

I understood early on it is mandatory to represent the message and topics I present to other women in business. I personally believe you may never have a second chance to make a first impression. This refers to both online and offline professional branding.

As a woman in business, if your appearance (i.e., hair, makeup, shoes, purse, nails, etc.) is not right, it is seen as a direct reflection of your professional destiny. If you have poor personal hygiene (i.e., body odor, bad breath, or other issues), that too can have an effect on how people receive you. This may make a difference if they are considering buying your products or services (or not).

A good personal appearance and good hygiene shows the business world how you look at and treat yourself, your business, and maybe even your potential customers or clients. Always remember your look represents you and the way your clients look at you as well. Carry yourself with confidence and in high esteem. How you view yourself is how others will see you as well. Remember, promote your brand from head-to-toe.

As a woman business leader, you have a lot to prove. There will always be others looking up to you for inspiration (family, friends, fans, followers, colleagues, etc.) for how they should present themselves too. By consistently striving for excellence in your personal presentation, you are providing a positive foundation.

In business, you brand your company by having a clear message on who you serve and how you do it better than everyone else. This leaves a lasting memory that will have your clients saying good things about you and your business well after your encounter with them. It also clears up any thoughts of uncertainty in the minds of those with a desire to work with you.

The lessons I have learned during my entrepreneurial journey and the challenges and obstacles faced now allow me to share many interesting and insightful points with you.

The next 10 tips are fundamental and ones I personally have found useful to maintaining a great personal and professional brand and image.

Personal Branding Tips

1. **Get plenty of rest and work out regularly** for mental stress relief, and find an outlet for the daily stressors that come with business ownership.

2. **Keep a positive attitude and an optimistic outlook** on your personal and professional future.

3. **Keep prompt timing with your scheduled meetings**, as this too represents your personal and professional brand.

4. Be consistent.

5. **Maintain emotional intelligence and stability**. Have tough skin, determination, drive, and the will to keep moving forward.

6. Remember, your network is a reflection of you. **Build and maintain relationships that are conducive to your business and life mission.** Surround yourself with people who represent 'brand you' at the highest level.

7. **Show leadership initiative** and your abilities within your industry to take chances.

8. **Assert yourself and stand firm** in your competence and confidence in your skills whenever you are faced with challenges. This type of strength is a vital asset which allows you to see each issue encountered as your opportunity for even greater success.

9. Scout and utilize **opportunities to help develop your business brand as you share your message with the world.** You will find helpful people and opportunities exist all around. Your community and network of contacts are only a few degrees of separation of offline and online supporters of your professional business cause.

10. **Work with a professional** as a part of your branding process. When you need an outside (fresh) perspective, a Coach, marketing representative, public relations agency, or graphic designer can each assist you with the continuous building of your ideal support team to elevate your business brand.

Get mentored. I have what is known as "Silent Mentors". Silent mentorship allows you to reflect on the lives and business practices of those leaders who came before you. It is motivating to learn about how these titans started out and to see where they are now in their professions and the business empires they have built.

A few business industry leaders and people who inspire me are Chick-fil-A Founder, Mr. S. Truett Cathy, Oprah Winfrey, and Mary Kay Ash of Mary Kay Cosmetics. They all have awesome stories I love learning and reading about. Success stories like those of The Pampered Chef®, Shark Tank's Barbara Corcoran, Paul Orfalea (The Founder of Kinko's), Sir Richard Branson of Virgin Mobile, and the stories of the creation of business empire giants like Google and Facebook all inspire me as well. I have read and listened to books and watched documentaries on each of these industry leaders and how they become successful in life and within their respective industries. I encourage you to find a silent mentor of your own who provides you with great advice and personal examples on becoming a well-known and established brand you admire.

Share Your Message

Social media platforms like Facebook, Periscope, YouTube, LinkedIn, Twitter, and Instagram are also branding and outreach sources to help share your personal and professional message. As others read your posts and see pictures of you in action doing the work you love, they are encouraged to help you spread your message and what you are doing throughout their network of contacts. This can lead to a few hundred or a few thousand new "brand ambassadors" who can help you grow your brand.

Other ways to build a better brand is to share your message through your professionally branded business cards. Your website, e-mail address, and online marketing. This type of brand exposure can assist you in catapulting your brand and your business' promotional efforts online.

A properly developed branding strategy should be to engage and build relationships with past, present, and potential clients before anything else. Start by showing your expertise and sharing what you know in small parts by doing things like blogging and sharing tips of helpful content or professional advice on a topic specific to your professional industry.

It is important to effectively communicate your message to get others onboard with your business mission. They will then become supporters of your brand as you share your passion with their connections too. Build these types of connections and relationships by engaging and interacting with people who support what you do.

Some of my past self-promotional success has included the front page press of local community newspapers and online magazines. I have been a featured story on television and a highlighted expert on-air with several well-known international radio stations sharing my passion and love for what I do.

In the beginning, barriers, or as I like to say 'opportunities', to successful brand promotion may present themselves in the form of not getting enough brand recognition or none at all. This is where you have to be extremely creative to generate "buzz" around your brand and make what you do and who you are rise above the noise of other 'attention grabbers' (like "the competition" in your industry) and stand out.

Here are 7 professional branding tips to help get you started:

1. Your company's brand and logo should use symbols that represent growth and transformation. Design a logo that stands out and represents the possibilities of doing what you love by impacting the lives of others. It should reflect what you will be doing throughout your journey as an entrepreneur.

2. If you can, feature a picture of yourself with one of your clients smiling and expressing the happiness and possibilities of what your company represents to them. Let it tell the story of how your business and your brand has impacted their life and the way they do business.

3. Use a consistent and specific font in your company's name and message to represent a certain style, class, and sense of elegance.

4. Your company's colors should also represent a deeper meaning for you. For example, purple is a color that represents royalty and elegance. Pink is a color that represents femininity. Red is a power color. And, black may be seen as simple, stylish and sophisticated.

5. Be known for using catchy or inspirational phrases like *empowerment*. These terms should speak directly to the clients you work with.

6. Create a signature phrase or tagline to help make it easier to share your brand's message. For example, one of my first companies was

known for the phrase *'encourage, empower, and entertain'*, as this spoke to what we did while working with our clients.

7. A key message communicates your brand, what you believe, who you serve, how you serve them, and what you specialize in specifically with your products and services.

One example could be getting solutions and results for your client's success. A personal example of my key message is the subtitle of this book, 'The TOP 8 Mistakes Women Entrepreneurs Make That Keep Them Broke, Stuck, and Struggling in Their Businesses and Inspiration for The Journey'. It communicates the message I focus on {business struggles/issues}, who I target {women entrepreneurs}, and how the "message" is delivered {inspirational}.

Your brand should inspire you, your team, and other aspiring business leaders to show them they can do it too. Here's to building a bigger, better business brand!

Let's Recap...

1. Your brand determines your business success or failure.

2. Branding is something you find, define, and own as a part of your professional reputation.

3. Your brand precedes you. Before you ever enter a room, it represents a professional snapshot, a picture of you and your business expertise.

4. A good personal appearance and good hygiene show how you look at and treat yourself, your business, and your potential customers or clients.

5. Your network reflects who you are.

6. Seek out your own "Silent Mentors".

7. Recruit ambassadors for your brand.

8. Set yourself apart by adding your own *you*-nique touch to your business!

9. You are your brand. Be you! Be clear. Brand you

Inspiration + Affirmation Checklist:

Place a check by what is true for you today. Circle what you want to work on. Make a note of it in your personal journal.

- ☐ I know myself and my true brand

- ☐ My brand is a celebration of my skills as a business owner

- ☐ I am confident in my business products and services

- ☐ My business is strategically focused on those who benefit most from my products/services

- ☐ My network positively reflects me and my business

- ☐ I embrace my online/offline community of friends, fans, and followers

- ☐ I have branded myself and my business to represent my true you-niqueness!

- ☐ I am my brand

- ☐ I take positive risks and chances in my life and my business

- ☐ I have selected my Silent Mentors who represent well what success looks like to me

PINK-Print Point 4:
Recruit.

Your fourth PINK-Print action step is to

recruit

brand/image ambassadors.

Remember, **the 5 empowerment tools**: **Spirit** {when a thought, word or idea comes to you. It is one of the purest, most genuine parts of you}, **Mind** {what you think and feed yourself through your thoughts often manifest in your life, **Actions** {what you DO speaks louder than anything you can say, as this shows up as the 'fruit' in your life and is often what people witness seeing you do versus what they hear you say, **Mouth** {what you profess out into the atmosphere often becomes your reality}, and **Heart** {when you are put on an instinctive alert by a small whisper or a gentle tug that comes from within}.

All five areas of the **spirit**, the **mind**, the **heart**, the **mouth**, and your **actions** go together to make lasting and permanent change!

Answer the following questions in your journal:

1. What are your top personal and professional branding needs?

2. How do you *think* you can use your skills to achieve more with your life/business brand?

3. What characteristics do you *feel* the most confident about in branding?

4. How will you *mention* your branding needs to others?

5. What will you *do* TODAY to gain new believers in your personal/professional brand/image?

MISTAKE #5:
Not Knowing When To Let Go

So far, you have gained a better awareness of the areas that can present themselves as personal and professional mistakes in your life and business. You see how procrastination is just an excuse to put things off for another day which may never actually get here. You've learned how a fear of failure (or success) can freeze you in a position that could potentially impact someone else's future. You can understand that it's empowering to face the reality that you are not able to do everything all-at-once or all on your own. It is even more powerful to stand out from the crowd and be yourself in your own brand. By doing all of these things and building the right support team along the way, you can set yourself on a path to potentially avoiding sticking points in each of these specific areas in the future.

While what you've learned has been helpful, sometimes you just have to see things for what they really are and know when and how to let go of what's NOT working in your business and in your life. When you continue to hold on to what's not working and wading through the waters of uncertainty you will continue to keep repeating a cycle and getting results you do not want. You can also learn to see things from an entirely different perspective. In order to get unstuck and avoid any unwanted results, you must learn to transition your life and your business in a new direction. I learned this lesson early in life.

I was a young bride (married at age 23). I took the leap despite the (unsolicited) advice given to me that I was not ready for such a life-changing event of this magnitude at such an early age in my life. At the time, I believed I knew what I wanted. So I went for it. It took only five short years for me to see the truth for myself. Looking back on the years of struggles and mistakes involved with the heaviness of a lifelong commitment marriage brings, I can now see what went wrong and when. Although matrimony was short-lived, all the "clues" were there from the beginning. I simply chose not to see them. Lesson learned.

Despite all reasons for entering into such a sacred covenant, I am now able to look back and see the reality of it all. I often think about how much easier things might have been for me if I had just taken the advice of others (my mother in particular) and not gone through with the vows. How much simpler would life had been for me? Something to ponder, indeed.

I have come to realize hardships are a part of life. Business life is no different and this is definitely nothing to be embarrassed about. Knowing when to let go is sometimes an inevitable process that is easier when you do not put up a fight and just get it over with already.

Truthfully, the only thing you should be ashamed of is if you have spent far too long faced with the same struggle. Do not keep allowing yourself to make the same mistakes and remaining stuck in the same position year-after-year. How many times have you ignored the whisper deep within you telling you and showing you signs something is wrong in your business or in your life? The feeling will always be there until you are ready to face the facts and admit it is simply time to let **some** things go. There is no need to continue to struggle.

Chances are, things are getting much worse than they have to or should be. It is time for you to ask for help. Make the decision today to swallow your pride and end this struggle so you can move on with your life. There are people waiting on you to walk in to the promises of your destiny before they are inspired to walk in theirs. So, let go.

There are ways to navigate your business and overcome particular obstacles and let them go. First, recognize you have a pressing issue that needs to be dealt with. Be realistic with yourself and everyone involved in your life and in your business makes things a little easier when it comes to letting things go.

Ever heard the saying, "*call a spade a spade*"? To me, this translates to mean in order to overcome a particular obstacle or address a specific issue, you have to identify ("call it") what it is: a personal or professional hardship, etc. Hardships are not always easy to identify (or admit). It goes back to one of the earlier mistakes mentioned, the fear of failure (or success). These mistakes combine certain levels and types of fear, and can keep you holding on to something that is not working for you for far too long. We all want to be successful, and many have a deeply rooted fear of looking like a complete failure to others.

Similar to what I experienced in my decision to stay married or simply let it go (I decided to divorce), at the beginning of your journey to acceptance, you may feel a bit embarrassed, stressed, and overwhelmed.

Admitting you are facing something that is particularly difficult for you to identify on your own can be frustrating. You may experience feelings of anger and a mixture of other negative emotions. When you do, this alone should concern you about where you are in your life and in your business as it relates to your personal and professional future. If you are constantly surrounded by problems and you are being challenged to achieve the results you want in your life or in your business, take this as a sign it may be time for you to move on to something else. Know it is okay to let some things go when the time comes.

Get help. One of the most helpful yet important steps you can take in this area is to get an outside opinion to help you work through this issue. Partner with someone who is good at evaluating and identifying the true issues behind your struggle. This will make it easier for them to relate to you and allow you to work together to get to the bottom of things. Is there a person in your life or your immediate network who is a good problem-solver and can provide a listening ear and a potential shoulder to cry on who may be willing to help you work through this specific issue? Who can you trust to help you get to a better and happier place in your life and in your business?

Your next important step is to see the **value** in having an outside opinion and a different perspective on your life and business issues. Find a competent friend or a professional who specializes in focusing in on what you are currently struggling with. This should help you get the specific results you need. Next, before making the decision of how you want to proceed with getting outside advice, it is best to decide how much time and money (if any) you are willing to invest in getting to the root of your problem. Then, as soon as you are ready, willing, and able to actively engage in creating the success you defined in chapter two, this is would be the ideal time to move things forward in working with a professional to help get you to where you desire to be.

.**Qualifications to look for.** Good professional help should be honest with you while also allowing you to freely share what is on your mind and what you are dealing with in complete confidentiality. Seek out a positive environment of support that includes a non-judgmental approach to listening to you and your issues. I recommend finding a professional to help in this area, but before you start your quest let's discuss specific characteristics to look for when seeking out assistance.

As a Business Coach, I understand my main job is to guide clients toward a solution for various business (and sometimes life) challenges. To help make sure my clients get their desired results and have a positive outcome, here are a few helpful tidbits of advice I give and you too can use to help make your selection process go smooth:

1. Be willing to be open about what you are currently struggling within your business and in your life.

2. Know what you want to focus on specifically during your sessions in order to make the most of your time together.

3. Be invested in staying focused and working to create a plan of action that helps your life and business move forward.

4. Be prepared to implement information learned.

Your main focus for getting help should be to identify your original business and/or life issues, and to help you plan your next steps for success. You want your chosen mentor or Coach to be available to you for one-on-one or group support to help you focus in on your specific business and life needs. (S)he should also sincerely understand the entrepreneurial journey when it comes to helping you with or in your business.

If you can, verify their history of knowing (and overcoming) the specific pitfalls in the area(s) you need help with. (S)he should not currently be where you are in business, or currently dealing with (or struggling in) the same area(s) where you are seeking help, guidance, or clarity and assistance in.

Also make sure they are rooting for your success. Be sure your chosen professional is only a phone call, text, or e-mail away to help answer your struggle-related questions and concerns throughout your pre-determined time working together.

(S)he should be able to share from personal business and life stories and experiences about what they've done to successfully navigate through their own past dilemmas. It also helps if they're at a point in their profession where they have mastered the details of the specific, challenging situation that you are now facing. A professional is not there to simply give out business and life advice of what they think you should do. It makes a major difference in the advice shared if it's been lived out (and overcome) by the person sharing too. It's even better when your input is encouraged and allowed, as this is your journey too.

With these specific qualifications to look for in a professional in your arsenal, you should now be equipped with the insight on how to find an exceptional industry professional who will see more potential in you than you see in yourself. The possibilities for your professional coaching/mentor relationship and success in your business and life are open and endless.

Just know, in the right partnership, your professional guidance-giver will want so much more for you, and (s)he desires to help you realize and manifest what you say you want for your life and your business. Your Coach, friend, or a mentor (or maybe all of these rolled into one) should consistently remind you of that too. His/her ability to lead you impacts your ability to achieve your goals and dreams. Overall, (s)he is there to help you truly own your own business and your life. Every stage of your business determines different needs. As this is the case, you and your chosen professional should also know when the mission of your session together has been served you will know when it's time, as your initial purpose of getting unstuck has been accomplished and it's time to move on. This journey alone will help you accomplish your goal. In the end, you will know when it is time to let go.

Let's Recap...

1. Identify areas of personal and professional struggles

2. Deal with the issues and stop putting things off for later. Decide when it's okay to move ahead

3. Do what you need to do to get (and stay) unstuck

4. Add a new member to your team for strong support and unfiltered advice

5. See things for what they are and know when to hold on or let go

6. Choose your safe-place for wise counsel and good, helpful advice for your life and business

7. Take an honest look at yourself and where you are now. Know what next steps to take for the road ahead

8. Know what is true for you today

9. Stop things where they are before they get worse

10. Recognize (and admit) your individual and business issues. Be clear. Set a plan for what to do next

Here is an Inspiration/Affirmation Checklist:

Place a check by what is true for you today. Circle what you want to work on. Make a note of it in your personal journal.

☐ I have identified where I am making mistakes in my life and business

☐ I have decided to stop putting things off for later. I am moving forward in this process

☐ I am un-paused and READY to make things happen in my life and in my business

☐ I am asking and seeking the knowledge and professional advice I need to get beyond where I am now

☐ I see things for what they are and know when to hold on and when to let go

☐ I know where to go for wise counsel for help with making tough life and/or business decisions

- ☐ I am placing myself in a better personal and professional position by knowing when to let go

- ☐ I will always listen to my inner whisper, which tells me what I know to be true for me

- ☐ I have put my pride to the side and I am taking charge of my life and my business

- ☐ I am honest with myself (and others involved) about my personal and professional issues

PINK-Print Point 5: Acknowledge.

Your fifth PINK-Print action step is to **acknowledge** what you need to keep or let go.

Remember, **the 5 empowerment tools**: **Spirit** {when a thought, word or idea comes to you. It is one of the purest, most genuine parts of you}, **Mind** {what you think and feed yourself through your thoughts often manifest in your life, **Actions** {what you DO speaks louder than anything you can say, as this shows up as the 'fruit' in your life and is often what people witness seeing you do versus what they hear you say, **Mouth** {what you profess out into the atmosphere often becomes your reality}, and **Heart** {when you are put on an instinctive alert by a small whisper or a gentle tug that comes from within}.

All five areas of the **spirit**, the **mind**, the **heart**, the **mouth**, and your **actions** go together to make lasting and permanent change!

Answer the following questions in your journal:

1. What area(s) do you consistently struggle with in your life or in your business?

2. How do you *think* you can get unstuck?

3. What do you *feel* is the best way to avoid making the same mistake(s) over and over again?

4. How will you *ask* for professional/expert advice on this issue?

5. What will you *do* TODAY to decide what you will keep or let go of in your life/business?

MISTAKE #6:
No Guidance

There are four types of guidance necessary for proper growth and development in your personal and professional life. Each has been found to be effective for avoiding the 'No Guidance' mistake. These guidance types are **spiritual guidance, self-guidance, peer guidance**, and **professional guidance**. Receiving guidance in each of these areas for your life and business are guaranteed to help you succeed. Take the time to seek the guidance you need. Once you are clear in each of the four areas of guidance in your life and in your business, you will be able to recognize your worth, your values, your beliefs, and what is truly holding you back from being the person and living the lifestyle of your dreams. This journey begins as a spiritual process, as it is important to start from within.

Spiritual Guidance

When you find yourself seeking a power source much greater than your own, start your journey to first find spiritual guidance. Some people turn to religious or faith-based institutions and organizations while many simply find a still, quiet place to pray, reflect and meditate. I have found music enhances and guides the spiritual experience. Get to a physical place that works best for you so you are able to focus specifically on you. Knowing where to go and what to do makes finding this type of guidance easier and well worth the effort. The spiritual guidance process teaches you how to go deep within for much needed direction.

I have found exercise to be the best route for aiding my spiritual journey. A brisk sixty minute speed walk is the perfect time for an internal quest. I use this time to seek, question, pray, meditate, and ask for clarity in specific areas of my personal and professional life. In this state, I am more open to a stronger mental and emotional connection. This often leads me to the self-guidance process.

Self-Guidance

The self-guidance experience encourages you to highlight your own personal qualities and characteristics. During this time, you are introduced to your "SOS". These letters stand for Strengths, Opportunities and Successes. A traditional 'SOS' is known to often represent a cry for help in order to be saved or rescued from something. In a sense, the type of SOS I am referring to can be used in a similar fashion. A self-guided journey is a spirit-led process that allows you to dwell internally on what makes you strong and brings on opportunities for success.

For example, one of my strengths is being a leader. This is a trait that began in my childhood. I 'played school' on the front porch of my home with several of the younger girls in my neighborhood. I was always the teacher or the leader. I graded papers, gave the "lessons", and disciplined insubordinate students. I was also my mom's eldest child and only girl. So, one could say I have been The Boss most of my life.

Being strong in this area has led to many opportunities to speak to, lead and guide women entrepreneurs from all over the world on how to be the boss of their own life and in their business. I have been successful at doing this. This scenario represents one example of my strengths, opportunities, and successes in life. Find a specific strong point of your life and business and locate your SOS.

Use this self-guidance time to re-focus in on your own personal strengths. These are things that make you great at being who you are and being the best at what you do.

Peer Guidance

If you are having a challenge coming up with your own SOS, find someone who represents the areas of strengths, opportunities, and success you desire to have for yourself, and use their success as a source of inspiration. This technique is referred to as peer guidance.

Using another person's success as a motivational tool for your future success is always encouraging. The person you choose to model does not have to be a well-known celebrity. He/she may be someone in your community who is leading the industry and taking charge of their own strengths and talents, opportunities, and successes.

Take time to reflect on areas where you have had success before and use this along with peer guidance as the inspiration you may need to create a vision for your personal and professional growth. If you are unable to complete this journey alone successfully, I recommend hiring a professional to assist you with this process.

Professional Guidance

Professional guidance helps you clear confusion. Working one-on-one with an expert is a great start to transforming your life and/or your business. During your time together, you may discover your deepest fears and your biggest motivations. It also helps to gain a fresh perspective of your life from an outside source.

A professional partnership and collaboration is an enlightening way to seek (and find) the SOS in your life. When seeking professional guidance, take time to define where you want to be and determine the most helpful method for how you want to be led there. Going through this process will allow you to define and easily recognize your own success when you see it.

My introduction to the business world included having several coaches who assisted me. I remember how great it felt to be able to share my thoughts and gain insight from having varying perspectives on my new business ideas and future ventures. I was surrounded by great women who had set aside time for me to help me launch and grow my business. They were committed to the process. My favorite part was I could share my thoughts and ideas with them so I could get them out of my head. They would help me dissect all of the pieces to the entrepreneurship puzzle and give me creative ways to help it all make sense.

In the beginning, I had the idea of making jewelry and handmade scented lotions and soaps. I called it fashion and fragrance. Once I shared this idea with my first coach, she told me I needed to narrow my ideas down and focus specifically on what I enjoyed doing the most, not just what could potentially bring me money. She and another business coach worked with me through a plan to help me see my passion was in hosting small group workshops.

Looking back on it, this process was priceless to me. Without that type of guidance, I would still be running around in circles with no clue on exactly what I should be doing with my business and in my life. Having the professional guidance these ladies provided allowed me to prune and fine-tune my business ideas and get to the heart of what I really enjoyed doing.

If this is where you are on your journey in life or in your business, seeking this type of professional guidance may just do the same thing for you too. Professional support combines planning with action that reinforces your goals and also aids in the accountability process. It is one of the first steps of many to start your journey to success. It also feels good not to have to go at things alone.

Next, be ready to put your ideas into action to help you achieve your goals and get what you say you want. The main requirement for finding your guidance is for you to be open. Open your heart to what you truly want for your personal and professional growth. From this point, you will be given what you need and what is best for you.

Once you research and seek wisdom on the best path for you to take in the process of finding your guidance, reach out and make the connection to the people and the resources available to help you achieve your goals. Finally, be sure you are at a place to make an investment of time, money, and commitment needed to complete the process. Be willing and available to do your part to make your outcome as successful as possible.

I encourage you to start the guidance seeking journey from within. Once you have the spiritual clarity and mental focus you need, you are well on your way to getting the answers you desire and avoiding the 'no guidance' mistake once and for all.

Allow your ideas to flow as you begin to get inspired by others who are living the success you have the will to someday achieve for yourself. Most importantly, get someone to come along on the journey with you throughout this process. It is always fun to have someone else by your side and on your team when you need a helping hand, and to celebrate with you when you succeed.

Let's Recap...

1. Get clear on which guidance-type you seek in your life and in your business

2. Finding guidance is well-worth the effort

3. Introduce yourself to your own personal SOS

4. Routinely remind yourself of your lifelong strengths, opportunities, and successes

5. Focus on your personal strengths throughout the guidance process

6. Use the peer-inspired success model for your journey

7. A one-on-one partnership is ideal if (or when) you get stuck

8. Invest your time and money in the guidance process. Be committed to your success and seeing this process through

9. Plan to take ACTION and reinforce your goals with accountability partners and a support team

Here is an Inspiration/Affirmation Checklist:

Place a check by what is true for you today. Circle what you want to work on. Make a note of it in your personal journal.

- ☐ I am clear on my guidance goals for my life

- ☐ I have the right guidance for my business

- ☐ I consistently seek new guidance for my life and my business

- ☐ I acknowledge my strengths, opportunities, and successes

- ☐ I am strong. Opportunities seek me. I accept each opportunity with success to follow

- ☐ I am staying focused on my strengths

- ☐ I have a success model for my life and business

- ☐ I welcome new opportunities of support for finding guidance partners

- ☐ I am ready, willing, and able to invest my time and financial resources, as I am committed to finding my guidance

- ☐ I am taking ACTION to reinforce my goals with accountability

PINK-Print Point 6: Develop.

Your sixth PINK-Print action step is to

develop and define

your next steps.

Remember, **the 5 empowerment tools**: Spirit {when a thought, word or idea comes to you. It is one of the purest, most genuine parts of you}, **Mind** {what you think and feed yourself through your thoughts often manifest in your life, **Actions** {what you DO speaks louder than anything you can say, as this shows up as the 'fruit' in your life and is often what people witness seeing you do versus what they hear you saying, **Mouth** {what you profess out into the atmosphere often becomes your reality}, and **Heart** {when you are put on an instinctive alert by a small whisper or a gentle tug that comes from within}.

All five areas of the **spirit**, the **mind**, the **heart**, the **mouth**, and your **actions** go together to make lasting and permanent change!

Answer the following questions in your journal:

1. What type of guidance do you *seek* [spiritual, self, peer, or professional] or all of these?

2. How do you *think* you can use your strengths and successes to gain more opportunities in your life and/or in your business?

3. What do you *feel* is the best success model for where you want to be in your life or in your business right now?

4. How will you *state* your need and make your request for partnership on this part of your guidance journey?

5. What will you *do* TODAY to take the first step in making this plan work and to complete it successfully?

MISTAKE #7: No Passion

Passion is what keeps you up at night. It is what you dream about most often. It is the idea that immediately comes to mind when you define true happiness for yourself. It makes you work late and get up before the sun rises to engage in what you believe you are truly called to do. It's the very definition of why you started your own business in the first place. Passion can never be taken away from you, and it cannot be transferred over to anyone else. When you are passionate about a thing, you do not make excuses for why you cannot take part in doing it. It also means you will always find a way to make it happen for yourself and others.

When you cannot imagine yourself doing anything else in life but this one thing, you are passionate. It is one of the main reasons you believe you exist on this earth today. It is when you say to yourself that no one can do what you do like you do it. Your passion brings a smile to your face when even the slightest thought about it crosses your mind. You smile a little brighter when someone asks you about what you do (or what you're passionate about).

You are exact and direct when anyone dares to ask why you do this certain thing and who you do it for. That is passion. Sometimes it is unexplainable. Every time you think about what makes you passionate, you feel your heart melt a little and a warm feeling of tingles and chills come over you.

Ponder these notable quotables about passion:

"Passion occupies your thoughts and motivates you into action, with no pay at all"
-Unknown

"Only sixty percent of women are living their passion."
-Anonymous

Believe it or not, I discovered my passion for speaking and sharing knowledge as I walked up on a church platform to give one of my dear aunt's eulogy. Strange, I know. But, this was literally my 'aha moment'. It was when I took that first step up onto the church pulpit and reached my arm out to receive the microphone to speak I instantly knew this is what I was supposed to be doing in my life.

Speaking to the masses and educating others on things I am truly passionate about. You see, my aunt lived and died with diabetes. I took it upon myself to read about and research the disease so I was enlightened and I then could share what I knew about the disease with the listening audience of attendees at her funeral.

I shared my aunt's life story and how she impacted the lives of everyone she knew. I also used this moment as a perfect opportunity to share what I knew about her sickness. I believe I enlightened listeners of my speech as I helped shed light on the signs and symptoms of the disease that affected my aunt's heart. I encouraged everyone to seek the expert help needed if they too had experienced anything like the illness that claimed my aunt's life.

After the funeral, I pondered all of the revelations I received in that moment. It was then I realized many of my relatives (known and unknown) were buried at this same church on the grounds where I was now speaking. I realized how I literally stood before my ancestors to speak, share knowledge, and embark on the path they had paved for me so many years ago.

This was a revolutionary moment on my journey to discovering one of my true passions. Speaking and teaching about what I know.

Passion is feeling like a kid in the candy store when you get to do what you love whenever you want to. If you do not have or are not currently experiencing that type of passion in your time life or business, it is time for a little self-help. To help you learn where your true passion lies, focus on two things.

First, focus on the idea your true passion is one of the reasons you believe you were put on this earth. It could be to impact lives, cook, design fashion accessories, or anything else.

Next, true passion is what you would regret not doing if your life suddenly ended. Think about it. But, do not think too long. Whatever crosses your mind in the first few seconds is usually your clue. Always go with your first answer.

Whatever thought just crossed your mind and brought a smirk to your face, a twinkle in your eye, and a skip to your heartbeat is what you are definitely passionate about. Whatever it is, do it!

No matter where you are in life or what you do for a living, if you are not passionate about it you must find a better way. Passion is all the things mentioned that defines what brings you true joy. It is not fair to deprive yourself of being your best and happiest self. You deserve to live in your passion every day of your life.

Here are a few things to note.

The signs of true passion are:

- ✓ When you do what you love and never question it

- ✓ When you eat, sleep, and breathe what you are passionate about

- ✓ When you notice how what you LOVE to do fuels and energize you

- ✓ When the work becomes effortless

To get to your true passion pay attention to how you feel after you do what brings you joy. This is often reflected in your drive and attitude toward a specific thing. Decide what you *want* to feel and how to get keep that feeling going.

Take time clear your head and narrow your focus. This discovery process allows you to find or fulfill your passion and truly live a life which pleases you.

To help you with the passion discovery process, take out your journal and use the following ACTION steps to get you started:

1. Name the top three things you love to do.

2. List three things you know you have always been good at.

3. What's essential in your life that makes it complete?

4. What do you feel you were born to do?

5. Why do you want this so bad? Why is this so important to you?

6. What has prevented you from achieving this goal in the past?

7. How will your life or business look different when you finally achieve your passion?

8. Who can you recruit to be your Passion Partner and help you stay focused on your passion and dreams?

9. Name a role model or an example scenario of your passion being accomplished in someone else's life.

10. What is the meaning behind why you want to do what you are so passionate about?

11. How does your passion impact the lives of others? (those around you, potential clients, etc.)

12. What are you definitely and most accurately passionate about in your life or business?

13. What makes you feel like you're not working?

14. If your income disappeared today, what would carry you on in this passionate lifestyle or business for free?

15. What feeds your soul in life? (it is often reflected in your business)

16. How did you feel when you first came to know your passion, or are you still waiting to discover it?

This fun activity and the insight shared within these pages is just the thing you need to inspire you to get started living more of your passion. Remember, your passion causes your lack of sleep yet it appears to you in your dreams. It is why you do what you do. Your goal is to keep it going and make no excuses!

Realize you would not be happy doing anything else, because what you are passionate about is why you believe you are here. You are good at something and you know it. Whatever "it" is causes you to glow from the inside out when you talk or think about it. You know the reason behind why you want to do it, and it feels right to you.

Your passion can be discovered in odd places or during a good or bad time in your life. Your passion makes you feel happy and free. If that is not how you currently feel about your work, you may be on the wrong path.

You can evaluate where you are by asking yourself the questions previously listed in this chapter to help you take action. Without knowing what is true for you, you may live a life of sorrow and regret. It does not take a lot to discover what moves you.

Find a way to do what you love. You deserve to be happy. You deserve to live your passion.

Get clear. Get focused. Get passionate.

Let's Recap...

1. Passion keeps you up at night

2. Whatever you dream about most often equals your passion

3. True passion can never be taken away from you or delegated to someone else

4. Make no excuses for your real passion

5. Passion is how you always seem to MAKE things happen for yourself (and others)

6. When you cannot imagine yourself doing anything else in life, that is passion

7. Passion is your meaning to why you exist

8. Your passion may be only an 'aha' away

9. Learn to recognize the signs of true passion

10. Your true passion starts within you

Here is an Inspiration/Affirmation Checklist:

Place a check by what is true for you today. Circle what you want to work on. Make a note of it in your personal journal.

- ☐ I have found my passion

- ☐ My passion and my dream is the same

- ☐ I acknowledge, accept, and receive my true passion

- ☐ I live my passion and I make no excuses

- ☐ I am passionate about making things happen in my life for myself

- ☐ I cannot IMAGINE myself doing anything else in my life or my business other than living my true passion

- ☐ I know why I exist and am passionate about it

- ☐ I am living my 'aha moment' with passion

- ☐ Passionate living exists for me

- ☐ My passion has true meaning

PINK-Print Point 7: Recognize.

Your seventh PINK-Print action step is to
recognize
your true passion in your business and in your life.

Remember, **the 5 empowerment tools**: **Spirit** {when a thought, word or idea comes to you. It is one of the purest, most genuine parts of you}, **Mind** {what you think and feed yourself through your thoughts often manifest in your life, **Actions** {what you DO speaks louder than anything you can say, as this shows up as the 'fruit' in your life and is often what people witness seeing you do versus what they hear you say, **Mouth** {what you profess out into the atmosphere often becomes your reality}, and **Heart** {when you are put on an instinctive alert by a small whisper or a gentle tug that comes from within}.

All five areas of the **spirit**, the **mind**, the **heart**, the **mouth**, and your **actions** go together to make lasting and permanent change!

Answer the following questions in your journal:

1. What are you most passionate about in your business and in your life?

2. How do you *think* you can enjoy your passion more in your life and in your business?

3. What do you *feel* is the best way to express your passion in your life and in your business?

4. How will you *state* your passion(s) to others on a more personal/professional level?

5. What will you *do* TODAY to make your passion your true cause in your life and in your business?

MISTAKE #8:
No Funds

It seems inevitable that as a small business owner, at some point during (especially in the beginning of) your entrepreneurial journey you will reach a point of having low to no funds available. To help you avoid this dilemma, I will share with you what I call the '**50-50 Plan**'.

Before I officially started my business over a decade ago, I saved fifty percent of the money I received from my "regular" paychecks from working a traditional 9-to-5 job to help build my pre-business inventory. Saving up for and purchasing things like office supplies and other materials I knew would be needed to run my business effectively was my main goal.

In addition to my paycheck, I invested the profits earned from additional income streams like consigning clothing, shoes, and jewelry with local consignment boutiques. I hosted yard sales and sold custom creations like handmade jewelry and fashion accessories online.

If you are able to, it helps to have other income sources outside of a regular paycheck to help you build your empire. If you can secure it, additional outside support from your family and friends is also a plus.

Speaking of family and friends, when you allow others to help you with meeting the needs for your business, consider the fact most people will expect *something* in exchange for their contribution no matter how small.

Whether they are investing their time, money, advice, or simply a listening ear, be sure to plan for giving each person some form of a "thank you" for believing in you and your dream to become a successful entrepreneur. It is also important to note before you can request or accept help with funds or any outside financial backing for your business, you should be able to ask (and answer) the following questions:

1. How much funding do you need? How long do you need it to last?

2. What goals are you trying to accomplish with these funds?

3. Where have past funds for the business come from? When did this financial source "dry up" or stop and why?

4. What or how much has been personally contributed and invested financially in the business?

5. What criteria should be looked for in an ideal outside funder? What characteristics should he/she/they exude (i.e., belief in your business and its mission, etc.)? Other than money, what else do they 'bring to the table'? Are these things enough?

6. What other professional (legal) hidden talents or skills can you use to potentially bring in money for the business?

Your answers to these questions will determine whether or not you are ready to go to the next stage of receiving funding for your business mission. Make note of where you are with this information and be prepared to share your answers to these questions with others who may be willing to invest.

If you cannot come up with answers to these questions, it may be time to reconsider your efforts. Sometimes low and no funds may simply mean it might not be the right time for you to start or expand a business venture. You may need to re-visit your finances to create a clearer money-making strategy before moving forward. Admitting you are B-R-O-K-E is often a harsh reality to give in to. Sometimes the financial truth is hard to admit and accept.

During my journey to build a successful practice, I have sacrificed houses, cars, friendships and relationships. In some instances, I have also said "No" to what some may call once-in-a-lifetime opportunities that might have led to larger income and a chance to potentially amass fortunes quickly.

Starting out, I made the personal decision to put off living what most would consider to be "the ideal life" or living "The American Dream" for the sake of building a successful business. I decided to pass on these "opportunities".

Since I was six years old I have known I was called to greatness. I knew my purpose on this earth would be larger than I could imagine. I also knew I was so unique I would have to create my own job. I had seen nothing like what I wanted to be when I grew up done before. From reading my children's Bible stories book, I imagined myself as the female Noah, called to save a people. I am now in the fortunate place of making my childhood dreams come true and living out the vision I have always had for myself. Who knew it would be through entrepreneurship?!

Business ownership has taught me no matter how much you plan, some things you simply cannot plan for. You have to learn to get comfortable with expecting the unexpected. The entrepreneurial journey is full of sacrifices and daily surprises.

Although many of my struggles and mistakes have come and gone, I often found it most helpful when I promised myself things in my life and my business would not always remain financially dreary. You should make this same promise to yourself. When you are most open about your financial situation and completely honest with yourself (and others) you will get the help and support you need. This starts the process of doing something that makes things better for you.

Being in business for yourself is no easy task. Having no money makes this journey even more lonesome. No money and/or no insight into how to get financial backing to continue to move forward with a business project can be frustrating. This is where you have to use your creative entrepreneurial mindset to get your 'hustle on' and make things happen on your behalf. Use the same passion which motivated you to start your own enterprise from the beginning and decide to stay focused and push through.

Seek out and ask for things like sponsorships and donations to provide support for certain aspects of business expansion and development. Getting help in this form allows you to save money while making money. The money your business saves through sponsorships and donations allows you to use the funds your business earns to invest in your other professional needs. Although the sources for getting things for free are plentiful, it is only a temporary fix to solving your "no funding" problem or issue.

You may think you are alone in the 'no money' struggle, but in fact you are not. You can only guess the amount of people who are "faking it until they make it", pretending all is well with their business finances while they too are barely hanging on. These are the same people you pass on the street or see online who are smiling and pretending everything is going good in their business, when in fact they are just days away from closing their business doors or facing eviction from their home, store, or office space.

I know from personal experience there is nothing worse than having your only mode of transportation repossessed. I have witnessed first-hand the embarrassment of having your personal property seized due to lack of or an inability to afford to "keep up with the Kardashians" (or the Jones').

You work too hard to get (and keep) your things, only to lose them because there are no funds in your bank account. It does not have to be this way. You may feel no one else understands but trust me, I do. There are many business owners who have a story to tell about what they went through, especially in the early stages on their journey to entrepreneurship. You are not alone.

There are resources in your local community for starting, growing and expanding small businesses as a way to help the local economy. Start with the internet and search for audio downloads, mp3s, mp4s, teleclasses, virtual trainings, workshops, seminars, conferences, special events, one-on-one and group programs, meetups, mastermind groups, books, tapes, books on tape, compact discs (CDs).

Your local Small Business Development Center or community college may be able to point you in the right direction for specialized training and certification courses and other forms of meetings in your area. These all share infinite opportunities for information discovery to use for your business acceleration. All of this knowledge exists to empower and enlighten you, the eager and willing entrepreneur. Allow these resources to serve as your guide and help you coast through your business, sustainability, and growth process.

Other Options

You can also "surf the crowd" with online crowd sourcing and crowd funding websites. These serve as effective fundraising tools that allow friends, family, fans, and followers of your business to show their support financially and help fund you and your business goals. Kickstarter and Indigogo are two websites that are currently in the lead as my favorite online platforms to put yourself and your business out into the marketplace to be supported and shared with others. Check out each of these sites to see what building a crowd funding campaign can potentially do to help assist you in meeting your business funding needs.

Getting funding for your business is important. It also takes consistent planning. Begin with an ideal minimum amount of the funding you may need in order to sustain your business and grow from month-to-month. Use this as a (necessary) starting point.

An effectively produced plan can play a significant part in you getting the financial backing you need. The PINK-Print you have been creating while reading this book can also assist you with potentially landing sponsors and other types of investors you may need. Have a clear idea of where you are and be willing to share it with others who may be able to assist you with getting a little closer to where you're going. Agree to re-visit your business plan over time (at least every 6 months) to be sure you are on track and to add any updates to make small revisions to your overall business/life vision.

Agree to have a meeting with yourself, and anyone else who your finances (or lack thereof) may impact (i.e., an Accountant or a loved one who may be depending on you) and update them about your growth and expansion goals. These are people who may also be in a good position to hold you accountable to the plans and goals you have set to help you move yourself and your business forward. You have to start somewhere. Start where you are. Use and appreciate what and who you have available to you right now.

Let's Recap...

1. Establish a plan to personally invest in your business first

2. Know what you will (and will not) give up in exchange for getting funders for your business

3. Before you ask for help, be able to explain how you have helped yourself. Plus, know how much you need and what it will be used for

4. Know your funding-funder criteria before you start your search

5. Surf the crowd and see who would be willing to 'chip in' on your business venture(s)

6. Reevaluate your timing. The time should be right (preferably ideal) for you to launch, grow or expand your business

7. Always have a plan, and plan to keep on planning

8. Seek additional online and offline empire-building resources

9. Create and follow your own PINK-Print you developed in order to know where you are and where you want to be in life and business. Revisit it often

10. Build your Accountability Team to help keep you on track with meeting your financial goals

Here is an Inspiration/Affirmation Checklist:

Place a check by what is true for you today. Circle what you want to work on. Make a note of it in your personal journal.

- ☐ I have a financial plan going in to business, and I am clear on where to begin

- ☐ I am willing to make the right sacrifices for my success in my business and in my life

- ☐ I am surrounded by supporters who are willing and able to financially invest in me

- ☐ I am confident that my ideal funder is out there waiting on me

- ☐ I am clear that this is the right moment for me to grow my business

- ☐ I have created my PINK-Print and I have an action plan

- ☐ I am investing in expanding my business financial knowledge through all available resources

- ☐ I know where I am and where I want to be financially

- ☐ My support/accountability team is great at helping me stay focused on my business and life goals

- ☐ I am thankful for the knowledge, financial support, and resources available to me

PINK-Print Point 8: Create.

Your eighth (and final) PINK-Print action step is to **create and invest** in your business/life dreams.

Remember, **the 5 empowerment tools**: Spirit {when a thought, word or idea comes to you. It is one of the purest, most genuine parts of you}, **Mind** {what you think and feed yourself through your thoughts often manifest in your life, **Actions** {what you DO speaks louder than anything you can say, as this shows up as the 'fruit' in your life and is often what people witness seeing you do versus what they hear you saying, **Mouth** {what you profess out into the atmosphere often becomes your reality}, and **Heart** {when you are put on an instinctive alert by a small whisper or a gentle tug that comes from within}.

All five areas of the **spirit**, the **mind**, the **heart**, the **mouth**, and your **actions** go together to make lasting and permanent change!

Answer the following questions in your journal:

1. What have you already personally invested in your life/business dreams?

2. How do you think you can bring other partners on board?

3. What do you feel is your best route for financial investing in your business future?

4. How can you clearly state the proper timing of your plans for your goals?

5. What will you do TODAY to take action in financing your business and life or personal/professional dreams?

The underlying message of this book is encouragement for you to build a system of support which allows for improved personal and professional development. The methods shared encourage recruitment of people and processes for manifesting your life and business dreams and vision. However, I heard a saying that there is no point to have a goal, vision, or a dream if you do not have a plan with action behind it to help you move forward.

Remember, the top eight mistakes covered represent areas that keep women entrepreneurs broke, stuck, and struggling in their businesses. If you choose to ignore the signs of these mistakes in your life and business, things will continue the way they are and you may have to face the reality of having to close (or never open) the doors to your business. If your choice is to heed the warnings this book provides, it is time to uncover the personal side of your professional struggles using your answers to the questions from your PINK-Print points.

Please understand you did not read this book by accident. There were ideas and undeniable messages that 'hit home' for you and your situation. Something may have struck a chord or hit a nerve and reminded you it is time to stop making these dangerous mistakes in your life and in your business once-and-for-all. Remember, someone out there is waiting on you to make your next move. Once you decide to do so, they will move with you to either support and keep you moving forward or be inspired to move forward themselves.

Remember to stay focused on the goals you have laid out for yourself in the parts of the PINK-Print to help you successfully run your day-to-day operations and for inspiration to start, sustain, or scale your enterprise.

ABOUT THE AUTHOR

Going from the death of her mom and a divorce (in the same day), the loss of a job and homelessness to building a globally impactful high-level coaching enterprise, Andrieka "AJA" Austin is The Socialprenista™; known globally as your super-savvy, straightforward, spiritually-connected business best girlfriend who truly understands the business woman's journey. Her unique speaking and teaching style combines transparency, authenticity, and her real-life personal and professional experiences sprinkled with biblical principles.

Her journey as a woman-led enterprise has now been well-over a decade long and is consistently rewarding as she gets to leave a legacy for the world by doing what she loves, and loving what she does. Ms. Austin has coached women small business owners for years and she avidly shares her time at empowerment events where she helps women showcase their expertise.

Raised just west of the Atlanta, GA city limits, here she serves as THE support system and resource for women entrepreneurs and has also been named 'Ultra Role Model', holds the honor of training and development leader of the year for her hard work, passion, and dedication to her profession. She also serves, supports and sponsors college leaders enrolled in business-based and entrepreneurial courses through her Virtual Internship Program [VIP].

You may have been encouraged, empowered, and educated through her books and business coaching programs, like <u>The Boss Of Me</u>, which helps women small business owners see beyond where they are to where they want to be as they confidently make connections through conversations that convert to clients, cash, checks, and credit cards!

Her coaching clients say, "She's a true Coach, because she keeps everyone in the game!"

AJA's transparent teachings of the top mistakes that keep women broke, stuck and struggling in their business and The Boss Of Me {aka 'The B.O.M'} message empowers and encourages entrepreneurs to #SpeakUp and use what they know, leverage their expertise, and increase their impact, influence, and income. Many are inspired to do so through her book, Secrets of A Socialprenista which is rich with accountability tactics to keep you on track to over-achieve your business and lifestyle goals.

Through her own empowering conversations and connections within a community of clients, she educates and engages with entrepreneurs through The Boss Of Me Business Coaching and Accountability Program that brings about clarity, focus, and accountability for women with a desire to elevate their vision and live out their God-given purpose via their business to support a lifestyle they adore.

Nothing pleases her more than to share her knowledge and to encourage other women entrepreneurs to share their expertise and grow their businesses. Her passion is helping women entrepreneurs live and leave a legacy doing what they love.

AJA is the eldest {and only girl} of three, loves afternoon naps, and has a penchant for plain restaurant-style tortilla chips. Pictures of her vegan/vegetarian-based recipes are gaining popularity on social media and getting better with each try.

She recently completed her studies and will be receiving a degree in Training and Development from Mercer University and she uses her platforms to tell her story of trials and triumph.

Visit: www.TheBossOf.me

Periscope: @socialprenista

Tweet: @socialprenista

'Fan': /TheSocialprenista

'Friend': /socialprenista

Link In: /in/socialprenista

Text 'Follow' thebossofme to 40404

What business leaders and leading industry professionals say about working with Andrieka "AJ" Austin...

"My sessions with AJ (The Socialprenista™) are phenomenal. She takes the time to listen to my needs and assess those needs with a wealth of information to assist me in expanding my platform. I am given the tools to create a very practical model and strategic plan. I would highly recommend AJ's program to any new or existing professional looking to take their career to the next level. You will definitely find value in the program and it is sprinkled with her one-of-a-kind, fabulous personality!"

-Alexis Lior, Life Coach/Speaker/Author

"Working with The Socialprenista™ is an enlightening experience! She has a clear plan of action, the right experience, and the background. With her help, I achieved more goals for my business in the first 21 days than I ever could have done in 6 months on my own! I am on track to increase my annual income! She was an EXCELLENT fit for what I was trying to achieve in my life and in my business. If you want a clear path for your life or business and need help putting your goals into action, The Socialprenista™ is the expert to help you do it!"

-Dawn Keene, MA Sustainability

"I trust the advice and guidance of The Socialprenista™. I appreciate her style, honesty, and NO EXCUSES accountability process. If you are a woman in business seeking to increase your impact, influence, and income, she is the Business Coach to help you get it done! I am a believer in her services!"

-Kascia Lipford, *Beyond the Front Porch*

"I see the success of The Socialprenista™ with other professionals and I trust her totally. I highly recommend her dedication, and unique ability to bring out the best in her clients! Thanks to her group coaching programs, I now have a plan to increase my income dramatically! "

-Patty Wenck, *Wenck Travel*

www.ingramcontent.com/pod-product-compliance
Lightning Source LLC
Chambersburg PA
CBHW070509100426
42743CB00010B/1791